EMPATHY FOR ALL

VERITY MILLER

Published in 2023 by The Rosen Publishing Group, Inc.
2544 Clinton Street, Buffalo, NY 14224

First Edition

Editor: Greg Roza
Book Design: Michael Flynn
Interior Layout: Rachel Rising

Photo Credits: Cover, NDAB Creativity/Shutterstock.com; Cover, pp. 1, 3–32 tavizta/Shutterstock.com; p. 4 William Perugini/Shutterstock.com; p. 5 M_Agency/Shutterstock.com; pp. 7, 27 wavebreakmedia/Shutterstock.com; p. 8 Ollyy/Shutterstock.com; p. 9 trofalenaRV/Shutterstock.com; p. 11 https://commons.wikimedia.org/wiki/File:A_group_of_young_evacuees_sit_on_a_hay_cart_outside_Chapel_Cleeve_Nursery_in_Washford,_Somerset,_1942._D9209.jpg; p. 13 Halfpoint/Shutterstock.com; p. 15 Abaca Press / Alamy Stock Photo; pp. 16, 20 SpeedKingz/Shutterstock.com; p. 17 AS photostudio/Shutterstock.com; p. 19 nikkimeel/Shutterstock.com; p. 20 Black Salmon/Shutterstock.com; p. 21 Luigi Morris/Shutterstock.com; p. 22 Africa Studio/Shutterstock.com; p. 23 BearFotos/Shutterstock.com; p. 25 fizkes/Shutterstock.com; p. 29 https://commons.wikimedia.org/wiki/File:Grace_Lee_Boggs_2012.jpg; p. 30 Vector Goddess/Shutterstock.com.

Library of Congress Cataloging-in-Publication Data

Names: Miller, Verity, author.
Title: Empathy for all / Verity Miller.
Description: Buffalo, New York : Rosen Publishing, [2023] | Series:
  Spotlight on a fair and equal society | Includes index.
Identifiers: LCCN 2022028229 (print) | LCCN 2022028230 (ebook) | ISBN
  9781538388037 (library binding) | ISBN 9781538388006 (paperback) | ISBN
  9781538388044 (ebook)
Subjects: LCSH: Empathy--Juvenile literature.
Classification: LCC BF575.E55 M56 2023 (print) | LCC BF575.E55 (ebook) |
  DDC 152.4/1--dc23/eng/20220617
LC record available at https://lccn.loc.gov/2022028229
LC ebook record available at https://lccn.loc.gov/2022028230

Manufactured in the United States of America

Some of the images in this book illustrate individuals who are models. The depictions do not imply actual situations or events.

CPSIA Compliance Information: Batch #CWPK23. For further information contact Rosen Publishing at 1-800-237-9932.

Find us on

CONTENTS

CHAPTER ONE

SOMEONE ELSE'S SHOES

Imagine this: a new family moves to your street. This family includes someone just about your age. Maybe you can make a new friend.

But when you meet them, you're surprised. The family seems different from others in the neighborhood. Maybe their skin color is different. Perhaps they speak in a different way. They seem nice, but … you're used to people who look and talk—and think—just like you do.

Differences can mean we learn new things!

In the past, many people have experienced similar situations in communities around the world. In the ones with positive results, one thing has been the same: people have stopped to think about what it's like to be in someone else's shoes. Understanding their experiences and **perspectives** with openness and respect is what it means to have empathy.

CHAPTER TWO

SHARING FEELINGS

Empathy is when you understand how other people feel. Empathy means relating to others with understanding and sensitivity for their experiences, beliefs, and **diverse** perspectives. You might feel sad when someone else is sad or happy because someone else is happy. When you're meeting that new neighbor, empathy is caring and thinking about how they might feel. And more, it's sharing those feelings too.

Empathy can help you learn to respect differences. If you truly feel how other people feel, you can start to understand why they feel that way. For example, you might understand why a friend's family **traditions** mean a lot to them, even if you don't share those traditions. Empathy is a starting point for positive relationships, responsible decisions, and respect for differences.

Sympathy and empathy aren't quite the same. Sympathy is when you feel sorry for someone. Empathy is when you feel the emotions they feel.

CHAPTER THREE

SO MANY DIFFERENCES

The people in our world are very diverse. We have different kinds of hair, skin, features, and body types. We're different ages and different sizes. We speak different languages and have different beliefs. We also have different talents, challenges, and ways of thinking.

Scientists think some nonhumans can have empathy too. Pets may show concern for human family members. Birds, dolphins, horses, dogs, cats, and elephants show empathy in their behavior.

We have a lot in common too. We're all human. We share needs, hopes, rights, and worth. Differences among people can be challenging. If all you've known is one thing, someone who looks or believes differently might be very hard to understand. This can lead to misunderstandings or conflicts. This has been true for a very long time.

Some scientists believe empathy may have developed as a matter of survival. Empathy may have led to early humans working together in better ways, including raising their young.

CHAPTER FOUR

EMPATHY IN HISTORY

The study of history often looks at **evidence** of how and why events and changes occurred. Empathy was behind many actions that shaped history. It continues to shape our world.

During World War II, more than 1 million children from England's cities were **evacuated** when constant bombing put them at risk. Many children traveled on trains to host families in the country. This was the first time many people from the two groups—city dwellers and country folk—had ever encountered each other.

Some of the city children were very poor. Their hosts had empathy for how hungry and poorly dressed they were. They wrote letters to newspapers and politicians. Many people started campaigns to help complete strangers. Similarly, many have responded to the 2022 crisis in Ukraine. Polish citizens provided food, shelter, and support as Ukrainian people fled their country.

Many well-off country people had no idea what life was like in the city. When they learned how hard it was for some children, they tried to help. This 1942 photo shows a group of evacuees sitting in a hay cart in Washford, Somerset.

Past social justice campaigns have been inspired by empathy. The history of **abolition** movements shows people banding together, sometimes driven by empathy for the horrors enslaved people faced. Some worked to make others think about what it would be like to be enslaved.

Frederick Douglass, who had been enslaved for years before escaping to freedom, spoke and wrote about his experiences to draw support. Angelina Grimké was from a wealthy white family that owned many enslaved people, but she left her home, family, and wealth behind to fight for abolition.

Pictures or factual accounts shared in books and the media have been a wake-up call for many people who want to help. Images and facts about tornado victims in Kentucky, hungry families in Afghanistan, or homeless people without shelter in any area may open eyes and hearts. Empathy and generosity often result in solutions and support for many needs.

People may not be able to fully understand the experiences, suffering, or needs of others, but empathy means they try—and they work to make change happen. Creating awareness is a first step for change.

CHAPTER FIVE

STANDING UP

Imagine that your new neighbors (from the earlier example) are now attending your school. But other students notice differences about them. Some people start picking on them. You can see the hurtful words and actions and feel compassion for your new neighbors.

You know that if you say something to the bullies, they might pick on you too. But if you have empathy for your neighbor, you feel what it's like to be attacked. It hurts! You can make a decision based on empathy. You can decide not to be a bystander and get involved.

In 2006, Barack Obama told graduates at Xavier University of Louisiana that people should try "to see through the eyes of those who are different from us."

"When you think like this ... it becomes harder not to act, harder not to help," he said.

In 2010, Barack Obama visited Xavier again and told the graduates to remember what happened when Hurricane Katrina hit New Orleans. He talked about how people stepped up to help.

CHAPTER SIX

WHEN WE DISCONNECT

Some studies have shown that empathy for others may drop as young people approach and begin middle school. Bullying, mean and hurtful behavior on social media, and even personal violence can increase as kids pass fourth and fifth grades. You might notice some people seem to care more about themselves, their status, and their goals than they do about others. They might not seem to care about other people. Screen time and digital technology can mean people might need to learn more social skills and empathy.

Self-awareness, caring, and kindness can push back against mean speech, put-downs, judgments, and **humiliation** on social media.

People might regain some empathy as they get older and develop understanding of differences, fairness, and social skills. Empathy can be taught and can be learned. Learning about caring, relationship skills, and compassion can help. Role models can also be very important.

CHAPTER SEVEN

PANDEMIC EMPATHY

Starting in early 2020, the COVID-19 **pandemic** swept across the planet, killing millions of people, leaving many others with health problems, and causing many issues with jobs and schools.

In some cases, the pandemic has highlighted empathy, showing cases of heroic people willing to help others. Nurses and doctors took big risks and experienced exhaustion, stress, and sadness while caring for sick people. Some people had the empathy to wear masks and keep their distance to protect those who were at high risk for serious illness. Many had the respect and empathy to do what was needed for others in their communities to stay healthy.

In some cases, however, the pandemic led some people to shut down their feelings. Some struggled to maintain their empathy in the face of so much continued suffering.

Empathy can cause stress and test the limits of our ability to have compassion while being able to take care of ourselves too.

CHAPTER EIGHT

TRYING TO HELP

It's human nature to sometimes disconnect when the needs of others are great. Still, many people, including young people, continue trying to change things for the better. They work together to stand up for their beliefs and take personal action for positive change. Many around the world showed empathy and took action to assist **refugees** from the 2022 crisis in Ukraine.

In many places, people welcomed refugees from Afghanistan to their communities in early 2022. They organized greetings and meals at airports. They paid for flights and provided housing. Some companies donated clothing and other personal items, while colleges offered scholarships and other helping hands.

Taking civic action, such as organizing protests, can be a way to draw attention to a problem and make people think about it. These people are marching to encourage accepting Afghan refugees to the United States.

In 2021, people formed Welcome.US, a not-for-profit organization that works to get government agencies, companies, and other groups to help these refugees. Among its supporters are three former U.S. presidents and first ladies.

CHAPTER NINE

BEING RESPECTFUL

Even if an issue doesn't directly affect you, if you have empathy, you'll want to help. Making the choice to help is the first step. Talk to teachers and family about what you can do. Ask questions and learn how to be a **volunteer**. Learn the best way to contribute by listening and learning from others who know the real-world needs and challenges involved. Read about a project or opportunity that would match your talents and values. Listen to podcasts to grow your understanding.

You can use your advantages for good. Listen to other people and back them up when positive change is in your hands. Learn about ways you can share your talents and strengths. Keep listening!

Next, when you get involved, be sure to really listen. Let people who experience the problem take the lead and show you how you can help.

You may have **advantages** that other people do not, such as family who will encourage you, transportation, time to invest, allies, talents, creativity, and other resources.

CHAPTER TEN

BE KIND TO YOURSELF

You can't fix all the problems in your community, family, or school on your own. And you can't feel everyone's pain like your own. Check in with your feelings if you need help meeting your goals or if you feel overwhelmed or frustrated. Solving these problems starts with being self-aware and keeping an eye on your energy and efforts. Taking care of yourself is important if you want to help others.

Sometimes empathy can be stressful. You may worry about what you experience and the effects of problems on real people. You can experience pushback from those who don't agree with your decision to help. Sometimes you can't help disappointing those who rely on you. Working closely with others and seeing the positive effects of your actions can boost your ability to engage with those in need and feel rewarded on a personal level.

Talk about your emotions or anxiety with trusted adults. Together, you can build a plan to find a balance in your efforts to make change happen.

CHAPTER ELEVEN

LEARNING AND GROWING

There are ways to learn empathy. One way is by talking to new people. This doesn't mean diving into other people's problems. Just be a friend and listen. Maybe work on a project with different people instead of your usual group.

As you learn and grow, you will practice and develop useful skills. You will become more self-aware by reflecting on your interactions with others. Managing your own thinking, choices, and actions will result in confidence in your ability to make change happen. Building relationships might be complicated, but practice helps you learn what works best. Finding and using your voice can change other people's minds.

Perhaps you will discover that you have ideas about other people that aren't true and need to change. Learn responsible habits from role models, friends, and mentors.

Someone who never has to use a wheelchair might not think about a lack of a ramp at school, while someone who does must consider how to deal with this every day.

Young people around the world and in communities near you have proven their awareness of what needs to change for the better. Working with peers as allies, they've taken action and stood up for clean water rights, education, solutions for the climate crisis, and much more.

You can work for positive change by communicating your knowledge of issues and arguing with evidence to back it up. You can speak to community leaders, write letters, post blogs, and design flyers and posters. You can follow or join groups that support things you care about.

Grace Lee Boggs was an Asian American from Detroit who died in 2015 at the age of 100. She understood the power of making a difference! Boggs taught that **activism** should be sustainable. This means it can continue.

Remember to make choices and decisions that keep you safe and ready to reach your goals for change. We can be the change we want to see in the world, but we can't do it alone.

CHAPTER TWELVE

THE WORLD KEEPS TURNING

One thing is certain: the world will continue to change. We'll learn about new differences between people, and the differences we already know may change. It will be important to continue to listen to others, learn, and build relationships.

Some people believe that empathy will be a major life skill as the 21st century continues. Technology means that the world will become smaller in some ways, and people may need to interact with more people who are different from them. Empathy can also help people look at problems and questions in a new and different way.

We also need to use what we learn about empathy as our future selves continue to deal with challenges. We'll know more tomorrow than we do today, and we'll need to continue to change and grow.

GLOSSARY

abolition (aa-buh-LIH-shuhn) The act of officially ending or stopping something, particularly slavery.

activism (AK-tih-vih-zuhm) Acting strongly in support of or against an issue.

advantage (ad-VAN-tihj) A condition that puts one in a favorable or superior position.

diverse (duh-VUHRS) Having many different types, forms, or ideas.

evacuate (ih-VAK-yu-ate) To leave or cause to leave a place of danger.

evidence (EH-vuh-dens) A sign that shows that something exists or is true.

humiliation (hyoo-mih-lee-AY-shun) Feeling very ashamed or foolish.

pandemic (pan-DEH-mik) An occurrence in which an illness spreads quickly and affects many people over a large area or the whole world.

perspective (puhr-SPEK-tihv) A person's point of view or beliefs on a topic.

refugee (REH-fyoo-jee) Someone who flees a country for safety (as from war).

tradition (truh-DIH-shun) A way of thinking, behaving, or doing something that's been used by people in a particular society for a long time.

volunteer (vohl-uhn-TEER) A person who does something to help because they want to do it.

INDEX

PRIMARY SOURCE LIST

p. 11
Young evacuees in Washford, Somerset, England. Photo. 1942. From the collections of the Imperial War Museums.

p. 15
U.S. President Barack Obama speaks at Xavier University in New Orleans, Louisiana. Photo. August 29, 2010. Abaca Press.

p. 29
Grace Lee Boggs at her Detroit home. Photo. February 21, 2012. Held for Flickr.